Lindamichellebaron

Rhythm & Dues

5th Edition

ISBN No. 0-940938-11-1
Fifth Edition
Graphic Design by Jorge Domenech
Produced by Unico International, Inc.

To Order:
Harlin Jacque Publications
P.O. Box 336, Garden City, NY 11530
516-489-0120   Fax: 516-292-9120

Visit our website at **www.Lindamichellebaron.com**

Activities for Personal Development

About Me

About Me

Although I started writing poetry when I was six years old, the poems in this book were written during a time in my life when I was trying to make sense of my world. I have always used the written word to help me think. I pay better attention to my thoughts when I write them down. I can revisit them and revise them. When I use the written word to support my decision making process, it allows me to make mistakes more safely. I can't cross out, erase, or crumple up my actions when I'm living them. But I can start with a new sheet when I think with my pen and paper. When I write, I have the opportunity to share my thoughts, and even be applauded for my thoughts. Below are some of my reflections about the poems you'll be reading in Rhythm & Dues.

Some People Think (p.3)
I wrote this piece because so many people seemed to have opinions about the "surface" me. They didn't know who I really was beneath the surface. They had no idea what was hidden in my future.

From the Giddy Up (p.5)
I really, really loved the young man I dated in high school. I loved his physical strength. But he was much more than that. He was intelligent. (That was obvious. He fell in love with me, didn't he?) He was a man who loved his mother and who tried, in every way he could, to protect his sister. Even back then I knew that a good indication of how a man would treat me was directly connected to how he treated the other women in his life.

Yeah Child...I Have the Blues (p.7)
I love the blues. The blues reminds me that the worst situation in life can be told with a sense of humor and a powerful rhythm.

Without Respect (p.9)
At one of my worst times, I decided to wallow in my misery. I sat with Dinah Washington's music and cried. Her music came from a deeper pain than I had previously known, and yet I responded to it by writing this poem and another called Refuse the Blues.

I Wish I Knew How it Would Feel (p.11)
This poem was written from my attempt to make sense of stereotyping. I refused to let anyone place me in a box.

We Don't Own a Boat (p.13)
I recognize this poem as my attempt to find answers from a higher source.

Confession (p.15)
Even when I write humor, I want to provide hints of another reality. Mine.

Fill'er Up (p.17)
One day, I just felt so good. It seemed as if everybody had something good to say to me and about me. Yes! I drank that up.

And Free (p.19)
One of my favorite poems is Maya Angelou's poem Still I Rise. I wanted to write a poem that spoke of a people "yearning to breathe free." I also wanted my poem to speak specifically to the shallowness I sometimes displayed..

For You 1 & 2 (p.21, p.23)
Some people did not consider my poetry poetic. I decided to name my creative expressions un-poetry.

That's When I'll Skate (p.25)
This poem was written on request. Vinnette Carroll was producing a play called *When Hell Freezes Over, I'll Skate.* I was one of the authors of the play.

Righteous Rap I & II (p.27, p.29)
I wanted to speak directly to young people, in a style they could hear. Rap.

Ignorance and The Rap (p.31)
I have never been impressed with unrepentant ignorance. Ignorance is forgivable as long as it is not a way of life.

Refuse The Blues (p.33)
I wrote this poem in order to get rid of my own blues.

Don't Owe a Dime (p.35)
This was a love thought that combined my child me to my adult me.

No Names (p.36)
I refuse to be lead into bankruptcy in order to fit in.

Sweet Stuff (p.37)
Again, this poem is a love thought that combined my child self to my adult self.

Blue Rendezvous (p.39)
This poem allowed me to enjoy the thought without having to act on what I thought. That was much safer.

Xerox and Love Me Some You (p.41)
I wanted to let the man I loved know that I loved him. I wrote this poem for him.

Dream Love Poem (p.43)
This was a special, special poem. I wrote this for my wedding day.

Benign Neglect (p.45)
I took this term, benign neglect, from one used by Daniel Patrick Moynihan in the 1970's.

Peek a Boo (p.47)
The games people play.

When I Do My Thing (p.49)
This poem was written after my prom. You can guess why I may have written this poem. The picture below is me, the day of my prom.

Raunchy Thought (p.51)
Well.

I Thought You Knew (p.52)
I wrote this from my husband's perspective.

Hope you enjoy experiencing my rhythms and dues.

Always,

Lindamichellebaron

Lindamichellebaron

About You

Use the graphic organizers.
They can help you think through the story of you. Draw or write your entries.
Share your thoughts with friends and family members.

(A) Create a spider web of your thoughts, phrases, beliefs about you.

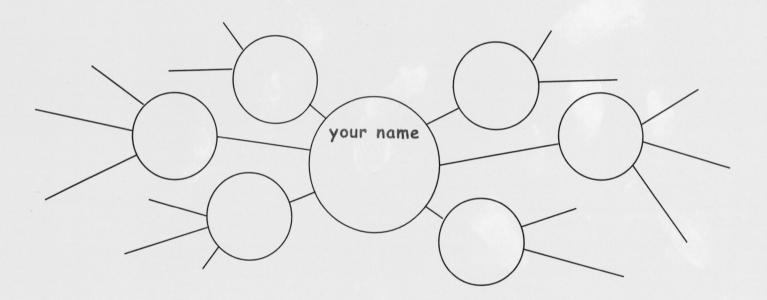

your name

(B) Create your personal timeline. Include experiences, people, places and things.

your past	your present	your future

Put your name in the middle of the circle.
(your actual name, nickname, or pen name)

Zynciah

YOUR NAME

· *Write as many adjectives and phrases to describe yourself as you can think of between the inner circle and the outer circle.*

· *Put a * next to the ones you like. Put one line through each of the ones you don't like.*

· *What can you do to change the ones you drew a line through?*

· *Look again and think about what you wrote. Make a mental note of the things you want to:*
· *continue doing (the ones you starred);*
· *start doing (the ones you can use that aren't in your circle);*
· *or stop doing (the ones you crossed out).*

Get some paper, and write your own "Some People Think..." about yourself. Add to this list all through the day for the next few days.

Carry this list around with you until it becomes a part of you.

From the Giddy-Up

I

When I first saw him
I knew
He could put those arms
around me
and keep them there...
loving me through a whole
lot of mess.
He said,
"I'm going to love you
despite your foolishness."

So, whenever I can,
I wrap my arms around him,
hold him tight
and SQUEEZE!!

II

Even if I looked like
I almost thought
I was going to think about
really doing some of the stuff
I talk...
he'd walk.

So, yeah,
I'm just looking.

Name some of the things you love about yourself.

I love my self because
I'm loyal and I'm who I
_am_

Give an example of what it means to love yourself or someone else unconditionally?

Honesty

Note at least 5 ways you can show you love yourself.

Note at least 5 ways others can show their love for you. Think of ways that don't cost $$$. Note at least 5 ways to show others you love them.

Sometimes you should put your arms around yourself and **hold tight!**

Yeah Child... I Have the Blues

Yeah, Child...
I Have the Blues

Yeah, child,
I have the blues...
I have the low down...slowed down
can't see the up
for all the down
blues.

I have the serious
no money...no honey and it ain't funny
blues.
Still paying the same o-life in the big
city dues.
Yes, indeed, I have the blues.
"Nobody loves me" wears my clothes,
and "nobody seems to care" shares my room.
Highs won't lift me off the ground.
I'm here about to "drown in my own tears."

Yeah Child...
I have the Blues

Brainstorm as many ideas as you can think of about what you want to do with your life right now and later, when you are an adult.

_____
_____
_____
_____

What have you done so far that shows respect for yourself? Detail your accomplishments. Each one counts.

_____
_____
_____
_____

Fill in the steps you plan to take to reach one of your goals.

You are not < anyone. You are > you even know.
And you are = to all of life's challenges.
< = less than
> = more than

I Wish I Knew
How It Would Feel

I wish I knew how it would feel to be black.
Not act like or be like-just be black.
Some puppet show no go!
Black with no strings attached.
Black without having to prove black.

 Sky don't act blue,
Grass don't have to kick _____ ...
to prove it's green.
Oranges don't have to define
the behavioral patterns of orange.
White knows white ... pure white ... light white
No conscientious make-up-let's pretend -
just is, because they say so.
Of course they have cleanliness and
godliness behind them,
but just is, because they say so.

I wish I knew how it would feel to be black.
So black I could stand
     undressed
     bald and
     silent
     and be black...
     just because
     I am.

So black-I wouldn't have to be beautiful.
So black-I could hide my pride.
So black-I could be anti or pro
whatever I feel
     so black-I could believe I am
     black for real.

Real black.
So I could know.
And know I knew...
     how it feels really feels
        to be me.

What are some of the things you do only because you
want to be like "everybody else"?

_____

_____

_____

_____

✔ *those things that make you feel good about yourself*

✘ *those things that aren't really you*

Close your eyes for a minute. Focus your thoughts on
you. Then freely write about who you really are and
how you can become better at being you.

(Don't worry about spelling, grammar or anything else.
Just write what comes to your mind.)

_____

_____

_____

_____

_____

_____

_____

_____

_____

_____

_____

_____

Celebrate your differences ... All that makes you so unique.
YOU can define yourself ... You create your own critique.

WE DON'T OWN A BOAT

Lord, when we first felt ourselves
    SINKING,
We knew You'd set us afloat.
But the water is rising higher now,
and we don't own a boat.

We used to be able to overcome.
We had a sense of pride.
We seemed to have some buoyancy, Lord,
through all we had been denied.

We gave birth to a flood of talent,
which seemed to encompass the earth,
Now we're being consumed, Lord,
by a leadership dearth.

Our tomorrows are dying on street corners,
dancing through knowledge.
They're trying to walk on water;
and can't read their way to college.

We need an ocean-liner;
and we don't even have a tug.
And I can't sleep for nightmares
where You just decide to pull the plug.

Before we leave without ark or rainbow,
could You just make it plain.
Tell us what we can do, Lord,
to keep ourselves from washing on
    DOWN THE
        DRAIN.

Because when we first felt ourselves
    SINKING,
we knew You'd set us afloat.
But the water is rising higher still ...
and we don't even have a down payment for
    A BOAT.

ABUSE

PREJUDICE

CRIME

DRUGS

What "boats" have helped you sail out of dangerous waters in your life? Friends? Family? A belief in yourself? Think of times when you were close to getting in trouble, but were "saved" by special people, feelings, thoughts, and beliefs.

WHAT HAPPENED?

_____
_____
_____
_____
_____
_____
_____
_____
_____

"MY BOAT" WAS...

_____
_____
_____
_____
_____
_____
_____
_____
_____

What do you think the folks from "back in the day" meant when they talked about "making a way out of no way"?

Confession

The only thing on my mind when I boarded
that rush hour train home
was how my boss worked me like he was absent
or on vacation the day slavery was abolished.
Me feet kicked like the mule we never got.
The train was packed like the ships that brought us over.
On top of that, it was mid-August cotton field hot.
I figured the Lord, knowing how tired I was,
would make my way.
That's when I saw this one seat,
Praised the Lord ... and started toward it
when a long black dress ran out from nowhere.

Well, I realize it was a sacrilege,
and I do hope the Lord forgives sinners,
though I don't know what came over me...
but I did race that nun for the seat.

And I won!

Guess I figured a nun is a nun ...
but a seat is a seat ...
and tired is tired ...
If she could run ... she could stand.
If the Lord wanted her to sit
he would have slowed down my poor tired feet.
No! He wasn't testing me - He just knew I needed a seat.
I ... sure hope I didn't blow my chance
        at heaven.

Humor can help you cope with serious situations.
How have you used humor in a serious situation?
Interview family and friends to find out how they have
used humor in serious situations.

_____
_____
_____
_____
_____
_____
_____
_____
_____
_____
_____
_____

Search for humorous anecdotes that can help someone
out of a bad situation.

Fill'er Up

Fill my ego.
Here's the cup.
I said, fill my ego.
I drink that up.

I'll smile,
and pose, and dimple up,
but just fill my ego.
Here's the cup.

I'll talk
and let my laugh erupt,
but just fill my ego.
That's what's up.

Say sweet words
that won't corrupt
but just fill my ego.
Fill it up.

I said, fill my ego.
Fill it up.
That's right, fill my ego,
that's what's up.
Hey now, fill my ego,
here's the cup.
Come on, fill my ego.
I drink that up.

Think of at least five things you can say to yourself to help you feel as good as James Brown when he sang "I want to jump back and kiss myself."

Think of five things people do or have done that "fill (filled) your ego."

Think of something you would want to say to yourself first thing in the morning (before you even brush your teeth) to make yourself feel good.

Now put it all in a cup.

Try another line from the man called the Godfather of Soul, "I feel good! Dooda dooda dooda do!"

... And Free

When I load the dishwasher,
Or clean with potions
that do windows plus
a whole lot more,
in rubber gloves which
protect my sculptured nails,
and decide between this and that,
for machine washed whites...

When I unthaw the frozen vegetables and meat,
Or heat the TV dinner,
Or just uncan some soup,
then complain about being tired,
after working nine to five,
in man-tailored suits
and toe squeezing heels ...

When I debate wearing my hair in 'fro
Or "African style" braids Or relaxed wet-look,
and contemplate what outfit
to wear and when,
while beating the mirror
in unleashed anger
for exposing my excess weight...
there is a part of me that spits out its disgust.

Where is the woman?
How did she tie herself
to fads and ads
of inconsequence?
How did she release herself
from the memories of her mothers,
who lived one choice?
One choice.
To deal and how
to deal...
and that choice
pre-natally determined.

Where is the woman,
whose enslaved, black,
cotton-picking, whip scarred,
head wrapped, body worn, foot bared mothers,
breast fed and cuddled
cotton colored children,
only to watch them grow
to enslave her own?

Where is the woman,
whose mothers' unmanicured,
unlotioned, unpolished hands
built a country for a full time job ...
embraced a family on stolen time...
and attempted to attract God's attention on the side?
And all of it for me
to live to be a woman
free and strong?

There is a part of me
that spits out its disgust...
and searches for that woman
strong and free.

_____

List or write about the positive characteristics or strengths
of your mother, father, grandmother, grandfather, aunt,
uncle, or someone special you know.

_____
_____
_____

Next, list your own strengths. Include strengths that are
already developed and those you are in the process of
developing.

_____
_____
_____

You have it "Going On." Use what "you got" and get going.

For You I

This unpoem is for you ...

For you who need new inspiration
from blocks of liquor stores
bars and holy storefronts
servicing different spirits
replacing all but candy stores
skimpily prepared for milk and cigarette emergencies.

For you who need new inspiration
to face dark faced tomorrows
blazing in living color
unappreciative audiences
for the sanctity of life ...
talking and living screen-style
dying Black Mafia style ... and
broadening their horizons
and Karate, Kung Fu images.

For you who need renewed inspiration
swept up like litter and cast aside
whenever cities need renewing
again in the wrong place
living on misplaced time.

For you who need understandings
of questions we thought answered
laws and statutes
amendments and "court decisions" ago.

For you who need new insights
to fight the new white sheets
with hooded minds
regurgitating unfreedoms.

For you who realize
this is not deja vu,
but a repeat performance of hate
personified and unabashed.

This unpoem is for you
who realize
hell is freezing over
and are making preparations to skate.

Aretha Franklin sings, "You better think, think about what you're trying to do to me."

Think, think about the way you interact with people you consider different. Jot down some of your thoughts about how they are different from you.
How do those differences affect you?
As you reflect on them, which interactions might you change?

_____
_____
_____
_____

Create your own anti-hate message.

_____
_____
_____
_____

"I just want to testify what your love has done for me."
   --The Parliaments

For You 2

This unpoem is for you
who have survived
who will survive
whose momentum cannot wait

for you who made first place
though they called you second rate
for you who were ignored
so they think you got here late
for you who know our history
and will set the record straight
for you who search for freedom
whose desire won't abate
for you who've been unloved
but don't need to practice hate
for you taught seven wonders
whose survival created eight

for you ... carried here as freight
for you ... able to take the weight
for you ... redefining your own fate
for you ... who prove us great
this unpoem is for you who are ...
have been ... will be prepared
to skate

BIG SURVIVAL BOX

_____

_____

_____

_____

_____

_____

Place in the BOX some of the things that help/helped you and/or your family or group to survive.

Freely write about survival techniques or whatever else comes to your mind.

_____

_____

_____

_____

_____

_____

_____

_____

_____

_____

_____

"Did you think I'd crumble. Did you think I'd lay down and die. Oh no, not I. I will survive." --Gloria Gaynor

That's When I'll Skate

Instead of to heaven,
they sent me to hell,
and then got mad
'cause I was doing so well.

Instead of burning up,
like I oughta,
I searched all around
'til I found me some water:

Now, in school, on earth,
I didn't do too well in gym,
but while here in hell
I taught myself how to swim.

Now the weather is changing,
it's getting chilly of late.
So when hell freezes over;
I'll skate.

What does "I'll skate" mean to you?

_____

_____

_____

_____

Study the people in books and the people around you to discover the techniques or ideas that seem to help them "skate." Write down the techniques and ideas as you locate them. Highlight the ones you might be able to use for yourself.

_____

_____

_____

_____

As they say, "When life gives you lemons, make lemonade."

Righteous Rap 1
(for our tomorrows)

When it's not what you plan
Against what you believe
When it fights against
Say No!

Some of your friends say
"Hey, let's hang out.
Why go to school?"
They tell you that's "fresh."
It's supposed to be "cool."
Tell them
You have another agenda
You refuse to surrender
You're reaching toward a higher ground
You don't have time to hang around
Say No!

Some of them want
To keep you from getting ahead.
They short circuit your learning,
And call you names instead.
Let them go!
You're not the one who's going to lose
Unless you live the life they choose
Turn around.
They're not going in your direction
So make a positive connection
Say No!

When he says how much he loves you
And wants you to love him too.
Says, "Let's get physical" ...
When physical is not what
You know what you should do
Don't do it! ...

You just look him in the eye
You don't have to be shy
Real love is much more, you'll find
Than what he has in mind
Say No!

Some want to turn you on to serious stuff
They promise to get you high ... help you deal
When the going gets tough.
Tell them you won't
Stick it ... smoke it ... sniff or snort it.
It's not your thing
You don't need or want it.
That stuff makes you a "self abuser"
You're a winner
Not a user
Say No!

When it's not what you plan
Against what you believe
When it fights against
What you want to achieve

Say What?
    Say What?
        Say No!!!

Saying you're going to say no is easier than actually
doing it. Write a rap that will help you "practice what you preach."

What is your definition of success?

_____
_____
_____
_____
_____
_____

Righteous Rap 2

(for our tomorrows)

Do you know who I am?
What I'm going to be?
I need some work
That will challenge me

I won't be happy with a "B"
That's not good enough for me
Show me the way to get an "A" ...

And don't make it easy
That's just a trick
"Getting over" isn't slick

Learning takes some extra time
It's not a "hip and a hop"
And a nursery rhyme

It's reading and studying
Not "boogie-ing down"
I can do more than dance all around

If you're not with me
Better step aside
To keep up with me
You need a forward stride

I'm going to step
And as I step
My head held high
I'm going to step
And as I step
Grab my piece of the sky

'Cause I know who I am
What I am about
When I walk -
You hear my body shout
I'm going to do it
Got to do it
Going to more than try
I'm going to make it
Got to make it
Get my piece of the sky

" I have plan a, b, c and d. Matter of fact, I have plan a to z. "
--Malik Wilson (a 3 year old)

Think of your plan as a map of where you want your
life to lead. Anticipate some possible roadblocks, or
remember some obstacles that have crossed your path,
in order to prepare for the unforeseeable. Make plan a, b and c.

Create a map of success for yourself.

Ignorance

Ignorance must become you ...
You wear it so well.
But I've seen you in little else
so it's difficult to tell.

What are you doing to make certain this poem "Ignorance" will not describe you?

_____
_____

The Rap

He glided over taking
 off his cap
 then proceeded to rap
 about the weather and
 what he did
 sandwiched around ... between
 did I want a drink
 and did I want to go to bed
 he said ... confiding
 (since I hadn't said yes ... I guess)
 that although his color might not be light
 his hair was right
 'Cause way before
 Geri Curled, Care-Free...d, Do Ragged,
 or even Fuller Wav...ed
he had "good" hair
The real deal...
If I wanted I could feel
his ... curly ... wavy ...
blow in the air hair ...
Like I shouldcare about his skin shade and hair grade,
But he was ser ee ous -
So when I said ... "No.
I'm not concerned, impressed, or moderately interested ..."
He replaced his cap ...
recanted his rap
and **dis** *ap* peared!

31

Are you judging yourself by using what really matters as a measuring stick?
☐ YES ☑ NO

Or are you judging yourself by using frivolous measurements?
☐ YES ☑ NO

Look into a mirror
__really, place yourself
in front of a mirror,
look into your eyes and then ...
talk to your inner self.
Decide to accentuate
the good
that goes beyond
what others see.
Talk to yourself,
you believe
you become.

Think of an adjective that describes you ___intelligent___
  e.g.: beautiful, intelligent, strong.
Write a three-to five-line poem that defines you.

Refuse the Blues

I won't get wrapped up in the blues no more,
I've been through all this before.
I've worn these same old lyrics too long
I can wear another song.
I won't get wrapped up in the blues no more.

I won't get wrapped up in the blues —
gonna buy me some running shoes.
—Run myself away from sorrow.
Won't look back, just greet tomorrow.
But won't get wrapped up in the blues
 no more.

I won't get wrapped up in the blues —
I can make up some better news.
I'm gonna quit all this complaining
Go on vacation when it's raining.
But won't get wrapped up in the blues
 no more.

I said, I won't get wrapped up in the blues
going to sunbathe in "I can't lose."
If I can't get me a man,
then at least I'll get a tan.
But I won't
 get wrapped up
 in the blues
 no more!

List the ways you keep yourself away from the blues
(thoughts you have, things you do)

✔ _____

✔ _____

✔ _____

✔ _____

✔ _____

✔ _____

✔ _____

✔ _____

✔ _____

✔ _____

✔ _____

✔ _____

Research: Ask people who seem to have a positive attitude most of the time how they do it. Read books about or by people who are positive. Note the things that keep them feeling "up."
Keep a journal with you, so you can write down what people say to you, and what you read or notice.

Be careful what you wish for, you just may get it.

DON'T OWE A DIME

SOMETIMES A SPARK
OF THAT OLD FLAME
   LEAPS
      INTO YOUR EYES...
HOP
     SCOTCH ES
       TO
YOUR
      TOES,
AND
     BROAD JUMPS
OVER TO ME ...
TURNING US
INTO ELECTRIC
CURRENTS.
AND WE KEEP THE NIGHT LIT,
FLOURESCENT BRIGHT,
WITHOUT OWING CON ED
A DIME!!!

Brainstorm some ways to put a spark in your own life.

_____
_____
_____
_____
_____

"Learning to love yourself is the greatest love of all..."
George Benson

No Names?

I quit trying to
fit my stuff into something
it's not about!
Cramping my style!
That "Ooooh la la" TV
is not for me.
I get no fame from
wearing someone else's name.
High heels and tight jeans
are not my scene.
My feet rebel ... my arches fell ...
my rear end squeezes the seat
like sausage meat.
  Plus ...
My pockets are not too pleased
about paying fifty dollars
for dungarees!!!

What pieces of clothing do you own that are really you?

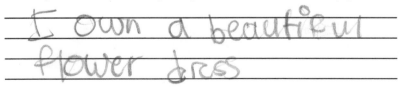

I own a beautiful
Flower dress

Make a statement about who you really are.
Create a mental map of what you desire to be.

"You can't judge a book by its cover."

Sweet Stuff

Every October thirty-first
my friends would turn
into clowns and pirates
and witches and princesses ...
and I'd turn into a glamorous gypsy
(with a black "beauty mark" dotting my dimple).
Then we'd "house to house"
until we were weighted down
with sweet stuff ...
which my parents, conscientiously,
kept me from devouring
all at once.

And when I saw you, just now,
looking like you look ...
(like some chocolate covered, caramel filled,
almond centered goodness,)
those sugared coated memories danced in
and wrapped themselves around you
All of you reactivated
my sweet tooth,
which at the moment
is probably carrying my words,
further than the rest of me ought to go ...
for although I'm trying desperately
to control myself
it's like October thirty-first is surrounding
me in goodies again ...
only my parents
are not
at home.

What are some things that you know are right and in your best interest - yet you let somebody push you into doing the very opposite of?

_____

_____

_____

_____

When can you use some of these phrases of the 1990s to help you say no and mean it?

What are some other phrases or expressions you can say to help you say no and mean it?

Sometimes your closest friends are not your best friends.

Xerox

The sister said
she was going to put you
into a Xerox
and duplicate you.

Smart move ...
as long as she
realizes that
        I
    KEEP
"the original"!!!

Why would someone want to duplicate you?

_____
_____
_____

Love Me Some You

I'm going to thank your mama and your papa, too.
I'm going to thank them both ...
'cause I love me some you.

I know there are some things
I do that I ought not to.
But that doesn't mean
I don't love me some you.

There are some things
I want that you won't do.
But I still have to say it.
I love me some you.

There were times I thought
that we were through.
I must have been crazy ...
'cause I love me some you.

So when those females
start talking 'bout
who ... what ... when and how much
they want to do
just tell them you have a woman
who loves her some you.

Recipe for a good relationship:

Put the ingredients you think are important inside the measuring cup.

Do your relationships have those ingredients? Which?

Which ingredients do you need to add to your relationships?

Dream Love Poem

When we get married, the sky will do it
just natural things nothing to it.
I'll wear a butterfly dress.
You'll wear a bluebird suit.
We'll fly to the wedding on cloth cloud shoes.
Then take a light ray for a limousine cruise.
When we get married the sky will do it
just natural things
Nothing to it.
The universe will cater to our natural affair.
We'll have tidbits of sun
and drinks served from the moon.
Then we'll eat at the milkyway
with a meteorite spoon.
When we get married
the sky will do it …
just natural things –
nothing to it.
Lightening will tap dance to
'Here Comes the Bride.'
It will be 'we love' tap tap …
'We love' tap tap …
Love and love side by side.
'Cause, when we get married the sky will do it
just natural things
NOTHING TO IT!

Brainstorm!!

How do you think nature affects your mood?
For instance: When the seasons change. When it's
rainy or sunny.

_____

_____

_____

_____

_____

_____

_____

How can you make your sunshine even though the
weather isn't doing what you want it to do?

_____

_____

_____

_____

_____

_____

_____

Remember: Every day is a good day if you are alive to enjoy it.

Benign Neglect

I'm really not ready to die of benign neglect,
though that's what's happening.
Living off of "when you did"
and "what you use to."

Maybe the loveboat
is just too steady.
Maybe the sweetcake
is over ready.
maybe the hot chocolate
has cooled instead.
Maybe the "need you" battery
is running dead.
Whatever it is,
I'm really not ready to die of
    benign neglect ...
So,
I'll rock the boat-
cut the cake-
heat the chocolate-
recharge the battery-
or whatever it will take
to put some more life in our love ...
    some more move to our groove ...
 some more nitty to our gritty ...
'cause I'm really too young to be killed by
    passivity.
So,
I'll harass and provoke,
needle or poke
you into making this a past tense
of what it is
or a present tense
of what it was.
'Cause the worse-est thing I've ever felt
is this soft
slow
death
by benign neglect.

45

How can you keep the enthusiasm going in any kind of relationship?

For example: with friends

     with parents

     with siblings

_____

_____

_____

_____

_____

_____

_____

_____

Why is it important for you to keep a relationship alive?

_____

_____

_____

_____

_____

_____

_____

peek-a-Boo

Even you must
realize there are no legitimatizing
words to excuse your playing
"hide and seek"
leaving me about to "rock a
bye baby on the tree top ..."
alone.
But anyway
your words ... my darling ...

"skipped to my lou-ed"
clapped "patty cake"
and "double dutch jumped"
through double handed
turns of your tongue ...
climbed their way up monkey bars,
and slid down slides
see sawed with themselves, and
merry-go-rounded each other.

I thought I could play
in your playground,
swinging when you swung,
doing what Simon said ...
But I couldn't
and I find myself past trying.
So after my having held on ...
perhaps too tight ...
being more playmate than lover;
it took some time to discover
I don't need to ride piggyback,
(even though they'll be two of me now.)

I can walk!

1. How do you make your decisions? ✔

    ☐ asking friends?
    ☐ using past experiences?
    ☑ looking within yourself?
    ☐ speaking to your elders?

_____

_____

_____

_____

2. Who has been most helpful to you when you are trying to make decisions that are right for you? How have they helped ?

_____

My mother / Brother

_____

3. Make a list of some of the things you value most in your life?

_____

_____

_____

_____

Take the time to focus on you and your life.
Keep a journal. Write your thoughts as they come to you.

Raunchy Thought

This is a raunchy, sexist thought,
that doesn't have a thing
to do with love ...
but your body turns the morning on for me.

All those parts of you
that got put together
just where I want them put
turns the morning on for me
and dances me through the afternoon.

And when I don't see it
there's no use in even
thinking about having a **gooood night!**

Jot down your unwanted thoughts.
Replace every one of them with positive thoughts.

−	+

I THOUGHT YOU KNEW

I thought you knew.
I thought you knew
my knowing you had my back
was what kept me
moving in the right direction.

I thought you knew.
I thought my hands, eyes, body
had already said it
and you read it
and understood.

I thought I didn't need
"I love you" taped to my lips
or tattooed to my tongue for you to know.
I thought you knew.
I thought you knew.
I thought
   you
      knew!

The way they act...

Fill in...
"thoughts"

Thoughts

What are some ways to read people's thoughts?
How can what you "read" help you to communicate with them?

Our Suggested Reading List

Lindamichellebaron "The Sun Is On" (Harlin Jacque Publications)

Iyanla Vanzant "Acts of Faith" (Fireside/Simon & Schuster)

Maya Angelou "Still I Rise" "Phenomenal Woman"

Susan L. Taylor "In the Spirit" (Harper Perennial)

*Eric Copage "Black Pearls: Daily Meditations, Affirmations and
 Inspirations for African Americans" (Warner)*

Janet Cheatham Bell "Famous Black Quotations" (Warner)

Carleen Brice "Walk Tall: Affirmations for People of Color"

Pamela Eapeland & Rosemary Wallner "Making the Most of Today"

Les Brown "Live Your Dreams" (Avon)

William Ayers "City Kids, City Teachers" (W.W. Norton and Company)

Drane Bunns "Songs From the Earth on Turtle's Back" (Greenfeld Press)

Niaui Giovanni "The Women and the Men" (William Morrow)

LouAnne Johnson "My Posse Don't Do Homework" (St. Martin's Jones)

June Jordan "On Call: Political Essays" (South End Press)

Zora Neale Hurston "Their Eyes Were Watching God" (Harper Collins)

*Maxine Hong Kingston "The Woman Warrior" (Alfred A. Knopf -
 Harper Collins)*

Audre Lorde "Zami: A New Spelling of My Name" (Crossing Press)

Mary Pipher "The Shelter of Each Other" (Putnam)

*Ruby Takanishi "Adolescence in the 1990's: Risk and Opportunity"
 (Teachers College)*

Revisit the poems in this book.
Think of a word or words for each poem.

Poem Titles	Your Thoughts
_____	_____
_____	_____
_____	_____
_____	_____
_____	_____
_____	_____
_____	_____
_____	_____
_____	_____
_____	_____
_____	_____
_____	_____

Poetic License

To be presented as needed.

The bearer is officially author *I* ized to: arrange, change, invent, improvise, regroup, rhyme or unrhyme any and all words, phrases, sentences and fragments -- for the purpose of painting pictures in the hearts, minds and souls of all -- in order to express thoughts, feelings, emotions and the truth as the bearer sees it . . . in the most original and creative style.

X _Zyne Poh_

Author *I* izing signature

Sign your own name. Only *you* can grant yourself this license.

Lindamichellebaron

Witness to creativity

Lindamichellebaron